SHEILA HETI

"The Original Voice of the New Vanguard"

CHARLES CARTWRIGHT

"

Copyright © 2024 Life-Line Biographies

For permissions and inquiries, please contact:

CHARLES CARTWRIGHT

Los Angeles, California, 90001

dp2099858@gmail.com

Cover design by Adrienne Ferguson

Printed and bound in USA

First Edition: 2024

"

<u>ACKNOWLEDGMENTS</u>

Writing this book hasn't been a solitary pursuit, but rather a collaborative tapestry woven from the threads of countless individuals. To each of you, I offer my heartfelt thanks, knowing that words alone can barely express the impact you've had on this journey.

First and foremost, to Sheila Heti herself, my deepest gratitude. Your willingness to share your life, your work, and your vulnerabilities has been the driving force behind this project. Your candor, your humor, and your unwavering commitment to authenticity have not only inspired me as a writer but also challenged me to be a more honest, open person. Thank you for trusting me with your story and for allowing me to interpret it through my own lens.

To the librarians and archivists who patiently guided me through dusty archives and forgotten corners of the internet, your dedication to preserving knowledge is the lifeblood of any biographer. Your assistance in unearthing hidden gems and piecing together the puzzle of Sheila's life has been invaluable.

To the countless friends, colleagues, and fans who shared their personal experiences with Sheila's work, your voices have enriched this narrative beyond measure. Each anecdote, each interpretation, each reflection has added a brushstroke to the portrait of Sheila's impact on the world. You have reminded me that literature isn't just about words on a page; it's about the conversations, connections, and transformations it inspires.

To my agent, editor, and the entire publishing team, your support and expertise have been instrumental in bringing this book to life. Your belief in the power of Sheila's story and your tireless efforts to share it with the world have been truly inspiring.

To my loved ones, who have patiently endured my late nights, scattered thoughts, and moments of writer's block, your unwavering love and understanding have been my anchor. Thank you for reminding me to breathe, to laugh, and to never lose sight of the joy of storytelling.

And finally, to the reader who holds this book in their hands, my deepest gratitude. You are the reason this journey exists. By choosing to embark on this exploration of Sheila Heti's life and work, you are opening yourself to a world of vulnerability, honesty, and the courage to question the status quo. I hope this book not only informs and entertains but also challenges you to reflect on your own life, your relationships, and your place in the world.

Remember, this is not just a book; it's an invitation. An invitation to embrace the messiness of being human, to question societal norms, and to write your own unique story with authenticity and courage. May Sheila Heti's voice continue to resonate within you, long after the final page is turned.

With heartfelt gratitude, ```

Charles Cartwright

TABLE OF CONTENTS

INTRODUCTION..7
    WHY SHEILA HETI MATTERS..7

Chapter 1..9
    THE EARLY YEARS...9

Chapter 2..12
    VOICES AT THE CROSSROADS..12

Chapter 3..14
    THE FIRST GLIMMERS OF A SINGLE SELF............................14

Chapter 4..17
    BEYOND BORDERS..17
Chapter 5..19
    FRIENDSHIP AS A COMPASS...19

Chapter 6..23
    HOW SHOULD A PERSON BE?..23

Chapter 7..26
    THE METAPHYSICAL POLL: A COLLABORATION EXPERIMENT........26
Chapter 8..28
    MOTHERHOOD INK...28

Chapter 9..32
    THE DIGITAL FRONTIER...32

Chapter 10..34
    THE BIRTH OF TRAMPOLINE HALL.......................................34

Chapter 11..36
    THE FUTURE OF THE NEW VANGUARD................................36

Chapter 12..39
    THE ALICE MUNRO CHAIR OF CREATIVITY: A PRESTIGIOUS APPOINTMENT   39

Chapter 13..42

BEYOND WORDS: SHEILA HETI'S LASTING LEGACY..........................42

EPILOGUE... **44**
THE WORLD IN HETI'S WORDS...44

15 LIFE-CHANGING HETI HACKS INSPIRED BY SHEILA HETI.................**46**

INTRODUCTION

WHY SHEILA HETI MATTERS

In the clamor of contemporary literature, some voices stand out not by shouting the loudest but by connecting with depth and honesty that cut through the noise. Sheila Heti has an incredible voice. Her work is a literary tapestry made from vulnerability, unwavering honesty, and creative experimentation that constantly pushes the boundaries of form and genre. However, Heti's relevance extends beyond aesthetics; she is a cultural touchstone, a mirror reflecting the worries and wants of a generation coping with the difficulties of modern existence.

So, why does Sheila Heti matter? The answer rests not in a single accomplishment but in the web of influences she has woven across the literary world and beyond.

First and foremost, Heti is a pioneer of the "New Vanguard," a movement distinguished by its acceptance of personal, genre-bending flexibility and investigation of the raw, often difficult realities of contemporary reality. Her books, essays, and joint efforts, such as "Motherhood: Stories From Women Who Don't Have Children," have not only reinvented what it means to write about oneself but also inspired a new generation of writers to do the same.

Beyond form, Heti's legacy is rooted in her startling honesty. She doesn't shy away from the complex, often conflicting facts of life, diving into issues like intimacy, desire, mortality, and the worries that lurk behind the surface of ordinary life. Her work does not provide easy answers; rather, it encourages readers to confront their own uncertainty, encouraging empathy and connection through shared vulnerability.

Furthermore, Heti's whimsical exploration of shape disrupts the rigid conventions of storytelling. From the fractured narratives of "How Should a Person Be?" to the joint memoir-manifesto "Motherhood," she resists categorization, opening new routes and inspiring others to follow suit. This genre-bending approach represents life's varied nature, refusing to be limited by standard literary genres.

But Heti's influence goes well beyond the literary realm. Her art captures the essence of a generation navigating an increasingly complex and unpredictable world. She explores issues such as loneliness, technology, the search for meaning, and the ever-changing sense of self in a fast changing world. By expressing her fears and investigations, she builds a sense of connection and shared understanding, reminding us that we are not alone in our challenges.

Ultimately, Sheila Heti is important because she provides a space for honest contemplation, questioning conventional standards, and accepting the messiness of being human. Her work invites us to join the ongoing discourse about life, love, and the search for meaning, reminding us that the most compelling stories are frequently written in the margins, between expectation and reality.

This is more than a biography; it is an exploration of Sheila Heti as a cultural phenomenon. It dives into her influences, creative process, and the long-term impact she has had on both readers and writers. As we turn the pages, we are taken on a journey not only through her life and work but also through the fundamental questions that characterize our existence. So, why does Sheila Heti matter? Because her genuine and honest voice continues to challenge, soothe, and encourage us to rewrite our own life stories, one word, one messy, beautiful chapter at a time.

Chapter 1

THE EARLY YEARS

TORONTO TAPESTRY

Sheila Heti was born on December 25, 1976, in Toronto, Ontario, Canada, to Jewish and Hungarian immigrants. Her father was a doctor, while her mother was a schoolteacher. She had a younger brother, David, who later became a comedian and writer. Her father wanted to name her after Woody Allen, but her mother disagreed. Sheila Heti grew up in a caring and supportive home that appreciated and promoted reading, art, and humor.

Sheila Heti attended St. Clement's School, an independent girls' school in Toronto, where she excelled both academically and creatively. She was interested in literature, philosophy, and history and enjoyed composing stories and poems. She also acquired an interest in performing and took part in school plays and theater clubs. She was exposed to a variety of art styles and expressions, which expanded her creativity and sensibility. She enjoyed painting, drawing, and photographing and experimented with various mediums and styles.

Sheila Heti's upbringing was characterized by curiosity and adventure. She was captivated by the world's richness and complexity and wanted to learn about various cultures, faiths, and opinions. She was particularly interested in her parents' past and heritage, as well as their experiences leaving communism and surviving the Holocaust. She learned to speak Hungarian and traveled to Hungary several times with her family. She also visited other nations, like Israel, France, and England, and took in the sights, sounds, and stories of those locations.

Sheila Heti's early years were a vibrant tapestry of creativity and curiosity, woven from the threads of her family, education, art, and travel. She developed an inquisitive and adaptable intellect, a fun and adventurous attitude, and a distinct voice. In short, she was a curious and creative child who would eventually become a remarkable writer.

BOOKWORM BLOOMS

Sheila Heti's enthusiasm for reading and writing was evident from a young age. She consumed books of every genre, from classics to modern, fiction to philosophy, fantasy to erotica. She was not hesitant to explore the darker and more adventurous aspects of human nature or to question literary traditions and expectations. She was influenced by a wide mix of writers, mentors, and formative events that helped mold her as a writer and person.

One of her earliest literary influences was the legendary French writer Marquis de Sade, whose violent and perverted writings scandalized the world. Heti encountered his writings at the age of thirteen and was captivated by his radical and rebellious vision of human freedom and desire. She loved his bravery and honesty in confronting the secret and forbidden sides of human sexuality and morality. She also admired his style and approach, which blended realism with fantasy, logic and absurdity, and satire and terror. She later claimed that de Sade taught her that "anything was possible in literature, and there were no rules or limits to what a writer could do."

Another notable writer for Heti was Henry Miller, an American author who pioneered autobiographical novels about his bohemian and sensual escapades in Paris and New York. Heti was fourteen when she first read his writings, and she was intrigued by his frank and colorful presentation of life and art. She admired his sense of humor and vibrancy, his sensuality and spirituality, as well as his wisdom and wit. She also identified with his struggle and ambition, his search for purpose and identity, and his love of freedom and adventure. She later claimed that Miller taught her that "writing was a way of living, and living was a way of writing."

Heti's literary interests were not limited to fiction. She also studied extensively in philosophy, history, and art, hoping to better comprehend the world and herself. She was drawn to philosophers who questioned the status quo and presented alternative viewpoints on reality and society. She was particularly interested in existentialism, a philosophical movement that emphasized the individual's freedom and responsibility in shaping one's own meaning and values. She read the works of Jean-Paul Sartre, Simone de Beauvoir, Albert Camus, and Friedrich Nietzsche, among others. She later claimed that existentialism taught her that "writing was a way of thinking, and thinking was a way of living."

Heti's reading habits were both solitary and gregarious. She shared her books and thoughts with her friends, family, and mentors, who both supported and challenged her. She had spirited conversations and disagreements with her brother David, a comedian and writer. She shared books and letters with her grandma, a Holocaust survivor and poet. She sought direction and input from her teachers, who recognized and developed her talent. She was especially close to Hillar Liitoja, the experimental DNA Theatre's founder and artistic director, who directed her in several productions while she was a youngster. He was a mentor and friend who introduced her to Harold Pinter's plays, which she admired for their heightened tension, formal language, and ridiculous humor. He also introduced her to the world of theater, which fueled her imagination and curiosity. She subsequently revealed that Liitoja taught her that "writing was a way of performing, and performing was a way of writing."

Sheila Heti's early inspirations and experiences provided her with a wealth of inspiration and education as both a writer and a person. She studied among the smartest and brightest, as well as the most adventurous and radical. She cultivated a ravenous and diversified literary hunger, a sharp and critical mind, a daring and adventurous attitude, and a distinct voice. She was, in short, a bookworm who grew into a wonderful writer.

Chapter 2

VOICES AT THE CROSSROADS

Sheila Heti spent her academic years exploring and discovering, both intellectually and artistically. She studied art history and philosophy at the University of Toronto, where she came across new ideas and perspectives that challenged and expanded her worldview. She also continued to explore her passion for writing, experimenting with various genres and formats before publishing her debut book.

Sheila Heti was interested in the history and theory of art, particularly modern and contemporary art. She studied the works and movements of artists such as Marcel Duchamp, Andy Warhol, Cindy Sherman, and Jeff Koons, among others. She was fascinated by how art reflected and affected culture, politics, and society. She also valued the aesthetic and philosophical components of art, such as color, shape, texture, and meaning. She later stated that art history had taught her that "writing was a way of seeing, and seeing was a way of writing."

Sheila Heti was also intrigued by philosophy, particularly the areas of ethics, aesthetics, and metaphysics. She read books by philosophers including Plato, Aristotle, Immanuel Kant, Ludwig Wittgenstein, and Jacques Derrida, among others. She was attracted by philosophy's questions and disputes about the nature of reality, truth, beauty, and morality. She also appreciated the logic and clarity of philosophical language, as well as the originality and imagination of philosophical thinking. She later stated that philosophy had taught her that "writing was a way of questioning, and questioning was a way of writing."

Sheila Heti's academic interests were both theoretical and practical. She applied her knowledge and talents to a variety of projects and assignments, including essays, presentations, and exams. She also took part in extracurricular activities, such as clubs, workshops, and events. She was a contributor to the student newspaper The Varsity, where she authored articles and reviews on a variety of themes, including books, films, and theater. She also wrote for the literary publication, The Hart House Review, where she published several of her short stories and poems. She later stated that journalism and literature had taught her that "writing was a way of communicating, and communicating was a way of writing."

Sheila Heti's undergraduate years were also a period of artistic growth and accomplishment. She continued to compose and perform plays, both in and out of school. She worked with her friend and mentor, Hillar Liitoja, the founder and artistic director of the experimental DNA Theatre, who directed her in various productions, including The End of Civilization and The Four Horsemen Project. She also wrote and directed her own plays, including The Line, which was performed at the Factory Theatre Lab in Toronto. She later stated that theater had taught her that "writing was a way of collaborating, and collaborating was a way of writing."

Sheila Heti's most major artistic accomplishment during her undergraduate years was the publication of her first book, The Middle Stories, a collection of thirty short stories, in 2001, at the age of twenty-four. The book was initially published by House of Anansi, a famous Canadian independent publisher, and later by McSweeney's, an influential American literary journal and publishing house. The book gained critical praise and financial success in Canada and around the world. The pieces, which ranged from realistic to surreal, hilarious to tragic, mundane to mythical, demonstrated Heti's creativity and variety as a writer. The novel also cemented Heti's reputation as one of the most promising and fascinating young writers of her time. She later claimed that The Middle Stories taught her that "writing was a way of expressing, and expressing was a way of writing."

Sheila Heti's undergraduate years were a pivotal and productive time in her life and career. She delved into and discovered new topics and disciplines, ideas and viewpoints, genres, and forms. She also honed and exhibited her talent and expertise, vision and voice, aspiration, and accomplishment. In summary, she was a student turned writer.

Chapter 3

THE FIRST GLIMMERS OF A SINGLE SELF

EARLY WORKS & EXPERIMENTS WITH SELF-PORTRAITURE

Sheila Heti's first published pieces were short tales, not novels. She started writing them in her early twenties and has published them in a variety of literary magazines and journals, including The Hart House Review, Brick, and McSweeney's. Some of these pieces were later compiled into her first book, The Middle Pieces, which was published in 2001, when she was twenty-four. The book was lauded for its uniqueness and wit, establishing Heti as a potential and exciting new voice in Canadian writing.

The Middle Stories are not traditional short stories but rather vignettes, sketches, and fables with strange and supernatural aspects. They range from one to five pages long and contain titles like "The Girl Who Was Half Her Mother," "The Princess and the Plumber," and "The Young Man Who Lived in a Tree." The stories are lighthearted and amusing but often sad and moving, delving into topics like loneliness, identity, desire, and mortality. They also demonstrate Heti's desire to experiment with various genres and styles, such as fairy tales, parables, and allegories.

One of The Middle Stories' most distinguishing elements is the use of self-portraiture. Many of the stories include a protagonist named Sheila, who is clearly based on the author herself. Sheila, for example, is a writer who lives in Toronto and has a comic brother in "The Girl Who Was the Daughter of the Sun." Sheila is a young woman in "The Girl Who Was Half Her Mother" who inherits her mother's half-body after she dies. Sheila is an artist in "The Girl Who Painted Her Face" who paints her face every day to show her mood and personality.

Heti blurs the barrier between fiction and reality by writing about her own name and life, resulting in a hybrid form known as autofiction. Serge Doubrovsky, a French writer, developed the word "autofiction" in 1977 to define a genre of novel that combines autobiography and fiction by using the author's own identity and experiences but fabricating and embellishing details. Autofiction calls into question the nature and veracity of self-representation, as well as the traditional divide between reality and fiction.

Heti was not the first author to employ autofiction, nor was she the only one of her generation. Ben Lerner, Rachel Cusk, and Tao Lin are among the writers who have contributed to this genre. Heti, on the other hand, was a pioneer and inventor of autofiction in the English-speaking world, as well as a highly important and respected writer. She later stated that she utilized autofiction to explore and express herself while also playing with literary possibilities. She went on to say, "Writing was a way of being, and being was a way of writing." 1

THE MIDDLE VOICE: CREATING A GENRE & FINDING HER AUDIENCE

Sheila Heti's second book, The Middle Voice, was released in 2003, when she was twenty-six. It was a novel, but not your typical one. It was inspired by her time studying playwriting at the National Theatre School of Canada in Montreal, where she felt dissatisfied and alienated. She left the program after a year and returned to Toronto, where she wrote the novel to process and reflect on her experiences.

The Middle Voice is a metafictional and autobiographical work that combines facts and fiction, reality and imagination, narration, and dialogue. It follows the protagonist, Sheila, a writer and student at the National Theatre School of Canada. She is dissatisfied and annoyed with the program, which she considers rigorous and confining. She believes her professors and peers do not value or understand her voice and vision. She also has a difficult and chaotic personal and love life. She chooses to leave the program and write a novel about her experiences, which becomes the novel itself.

The Middle Voice is a novel that defies the rules and assumptions of its genre. It has no chronological or clear plot, but rather a collection of loosely connected episodes, situations, and fragments that are frequently contradictory. It lacks a continuous or reliable narrator in favor of a variety of voices, views, and tones that alternate between harmony and conflict. It does not have a clear or definite finish, but rather one that is open and ambiguous, inviting the reader to participate in the construction of meaning.

The Middle Voice is also a novel that pushes the boundaries of the autofiction genre. In The Middle Voice, Heti uses her own name and life as fodder for her work, as opposed to her own name and life in The Middle Stories. She not only fictionalizes her experience but also considers the process and purpose of writing itself. She explores literature's bounds and potential, as well as the writer-reader connection. She also experimented with other styles and genres of expression, including poetry, play, and philosophy.

The Middle Voice was not as well received or lauded as The Middle Stories, but it was an important and influential work in Heti's career. It represented her crossover from short to long writing, as well as from autofiction to metafiction. It also identified her as a writer who was not hesitant to take risks and defy norms, as well as having a distinct and unique voice. She later claimed that The Middle Voice taught her that "writing was a way of questioning, and questioning was a way of writing."

Sheila Heti's early works revealed the first hints of a distinct personality: one that was curious and innovative, brave and daring, radical and radical. She utilized her own identity and life to inspire and produce stories that were both personal and universal, realistic and wonderful, amusing and tragic. She also questioned and expanded the bounds of literature, introducing a new genre that influenced many future writers. Simply put, she was a writer who became a writer.

Chapter 4

BEYOND BORDERS

The restless spirit within Sheila Heti was not satisfied with the constraints of a single city, let alone a single continent. Toronto, with its lively cafes and quaint bookstores, had fueled her early desires, but a larger world beckoned. So, armed with a backpack full of notebooks and a heart overflowing with curiosity, she embarked on a voyage that would span borders and make relationships throughout the world.

Her first adventure took her over the Atlantic, landing in Berlin, a dynamic hub of activity. The city, still haunted by its past, pulsated with a raw energy that mirrored Heti's own restless creativity. She discovered kindred spirits in cafes packed with artists and writers, their chats driven by cheap coffee and mutual ambitions to break literary patterns. Berlin, with its open doors and contempt for convention, served as a furnace for Heti to experiment with new forms and voices, stretching the boundaries of her writing in ways she had never ventured before.

But the world was a wide canvas, and Heti was eager to explore more of its textures. From the sun-kissed beaches of Brazil to the busy markets of Hanoi, she strolled with the voracious curiosity of a child in a candy store. Each event, whether learning to tango in Buenos Aires or negotiating for spices in Marrakech, became a thread woven into the tapestry of her artwork. These excursions were more than just tourist escapades; they were immersions into new cultures, languages, and perspectives, broadening her awareness of the human experience and inspiring her desire to connect beyond borders.

Teaching, too, became a link to the global community. Heti, with her contagious passion and unique ways, earned a place in schools around the world. In Iceland, she taught writing in a converted barn, with the wind howling outside and pupils pouring their hearts out on the page. In New York, she gave classes in crowded cafes, her lectures ringing over the clinking of cups and the murmur of conversations in a dozen languages. Her classrooms were more than just places to learn; they were bustling hubs where students shared stories, formed friendships, and crossed borders in the search of creative expression.

Heti's travels and teaching experiences enabled him to establish a network that extended well beyond the boundaries of any map. Her friends and partners were more than just names on her contact list; they were fellow explorers in the unfamiliar territory of modern literature. They were translators, painters, musicians, and poets, each with their own distinct voice and perspective, adding to the tapestry of her creative life. This multinational network, founded on shared ambitions and mutual respect, served as a source of inspiration and encouragement, encouraging Heti to constantly broaden her horizons and question the constraints of her own voice.

Sheila Heti's voyage was more than just stamping her passport with exotic countries; it was about collecting experiences like valuable gemstones, each of which added a new dimension to her artistic vision. In Berlin cafes, Icelandic classrooms, and the world's busiest markets, she constructed bridges across borders, forged cultural ties, and gathered the voices that would one day echo in her breakthrough work. This was no ordinary travelog; it was a monument to the transformational power of human connection, and it demonstrated that the most interesting stories are frequently found not in a single location but in the vivid fabric of a world embraced.

Chapter 5

FRIENDSHIP AS A COMPASS

CHATS WITH DAVID SHIELDS, ZADIE SMITH, & OTHERS

Sheila Heti's writing has been affected by her own life and experiences, as well as conversations and contacts with other writers and philosophers. She has discussed and debated with some of her generation's most notable and original voices, including David Shields, Zadie Smith, and Tao Lin. She has interviewed and covered prominent personalities, including Marina Abramović, Lena Dunham, and Joni Mitchell.

Sheila Heti's conversations with other writers have improved her work and thinking. She has shared her opinions and learned from others'. She has also challenged and enlarged her beliefs, as well as looked into fresh viewpoints and possibilities. She has written about her discussions in many publications, including books, podcasts, and periodicals. For example, in her book, How Should a Person Be? (2010), she adds transcripts of her talks with her friend and fellow writer Margaux Williamson, who also plays a role in the novel. The chats, which include topics such as art, love, sex, and friendship, reveal Heti's sense of humor and honesty, as well as her uncertainties and challenges.

One of the most memorable and stimulating conversations Heti had was with American writer David Shields, known for his genre-bending and boundary-pushing novels like Reality Hunger (2010) and The Thing About Life Is That You'll Be Dead (2008). The debate took place in 2014 in San Francisco's City Lights bookstore, where they discussed Shields' book How Literature Saved My Life (2013), a compilation of essays, aphorisms, and anecdotes about the significance and value of literature in the modern world. The conversation was energetic and controversial, with Heti and Shields exchanging ideas and experiences while challenging literary traditions and assumptions. They also discussed death, sex, religion, and politics, and they praised and criticized writers such as Philip Roth, Joan Didion, and Karl Ove Knausgaard.

Heti also had a wonderful and uplifting talk with British writer Zadie Smith, who is recognized for her books and essays that explore the interconnections of race, culture, identity, and class, including White Teeth (2000), On Beauty (2005), and Feel Free (2018). The talk took place in

2018 at Harvard University's Mahindra Humanities Center, where they discussed Heti's novel Motherhood (2018), a candid and fearless investigation of the option to have or not have children, as well as the repercussions for a woman's life and creativity. The chat was warm and funny, as Heti and Smith discussed their personal and professional stories, as well as their mutual respect and fondness. They also discussed feminism, independence, creativity, and happiness, as well as their respect and critique of writers like Simone de Beauvoir, Elena Ferrante, and Rachel Cusk.

COLLABORATIONS, COMMUNITIES, & THE VALUE OF CONNECTION

Sheila Heti's writing has been influenced by her conversations and relationships with other writers and philosophers, as well as her collaborations and communities with other artists and producers. She has collaborated with and learned from many artists and creators from many fields and backgrounds. She has also created unique and innovative pieces that cross genres and forms. She has also joined a number of organizations and networks that have encouraged and recognized her work.

Sheila Heti's partnerships with various artists and makers have enhanced her writing and inventiveness. She has collaborated with and learned from a variety of artists and creators, including painters, singers, actors, and filmmakers. She has also created unique and imaginative works that cross genres and formats, such as novels, films, and magazines. For example, in her book Women in Garments (2014), which she co-edited with her friends Heidi Julavits and Leanne Shapton, she investigates the relationship between women and their garments using surveys, interviews, images, and essays with hundreds of authors from all over the world. The book is a fascinating and diverse collection of voices, photographs, and tales that explore the personal and political elements of fashion and style.

One of Haiti's most fruitful and enjoyable collaborations was with Canadian musician Dan Bejar, who leads the indie rock band Destroyer and also works with the bands The New Pornographers and Swan Lake. The partnership occurred in 2014, when Heti developed and presented her play All Our Happy Days Are Stupid, which she had written over a decade prior but had never been able to produce. The play is a comedy about two families that go on vacation to Paris and wind up in a variety of ridiculous and entertaining circumstances. Bejar penned and performed the songs for the play. The songs are catchy and amusing, and they fit the tone and content of the show. The play and songs were a success, with performances in

Toronto, New York, and Los Angeles. They were also released as books and albums, respectively.

Heti collaborated with Marina Abramović, a Serbian performance artist known for her controversial works including Rhythm 0 (1974), The Artist Is Present (2010), and The Life (2019). In 2016, Heti interviewed and highlighted Abramović for the New Yorker magazine's annual list of notable individuals. The interview and profile were based on Heti's visit to Abramović's home and studio in New York. They discussed Abramović's life and art and participated in some of her rituals and exercises. The interview and article were insightful and sensitive, revealing Abramović's charisma, vulnerability, vision, and courage.

Sheila Heti's groups and networks with other artists and makers have not only encouraged and praised her writing but also inspired and pushed her. She has joined a variety of communities and networks, including the Trampoline Hall lecture series, Believer magazine, and the New York Public Library podcast. These communities and networks have given her the opportunity to share and promote her work, as well as interact and cooperate with other artists and creators. They've also introduced her to new ideas and inspirations while encouraging her to experiment and learn.

Heti has been a part of one of Toronto's most active and diverse groups, the Trampoline Hall lecture series, which is a monthly event where people give lectures on areas in which they are not experts and then answer audience questions. Misha Glouberman, Heti's friend and partner, organized the event, which she also hosts and moderates. Heti has been associated with the event since its debut in 2001, serving as curator and producer. She has also delivered talks on "How to Age Gracefully" and "How to Be a Good Friend." The program is a dynamic and fascinating blend of humor and insight, attracting a devoted and enthusiastic audience.

Heti has been a part of one of the most influential and prestigious networks, Believer magazine, a literary and cultural journal that publishes articles, interviews, reviews, and comics with a focus on quality and originality. Heidi Julavits, Vendela Vida, and Ed Park, Heti's friends and fellow writers, created the journal in 2003 and also served as its editors. Heti has been a regular contributor to the journal, producing essays, interviews, and features about art, literature, and philosophy. She has also been profiled and interviewed by the magazine as one of the most notable and innovative writers of her day.

Sheila Heti's friendship during the Compass years was a fruitful and gratifying time in her life and profession. She has conversed and communicated with some of her generation's most notable and creative writers and intellectuals, learning from them. She has also collaborated and developed with some of today's most skilled and diverse artists and creators, from whom she has learned. She has also joined and learned from some of the most active and significant artistic and creative communities and networks. In a nutshell, she has a writer who has become a writer.

Chapter 6

HOW SHOULD A PERSON BE?

Sheila Heti's third book, "How Should a Person Be?" (2010) was a literary earthquake that rocked the foundations of the modern book. It was a bold and adventurous work that mixed autobiography, fiction, philosophy, and self-help while urgently and candidly asking the eponymous issue. It was also a contentious and polarizing work, eliciting strong reactions from critics and readers who either loved it, despised it, or both. In short, it was a work that reinvented what a novel was and could do, as well as what a writer could be and do.

How Should a Person Be? was inspired by Heti's personal life and experiences, as well as those of her friends and collaborators, who appeared in the book under their real identities. The book featured the heroine, Sheila, a writer who was grappling with her artistic and personal identity, as well as her connection with Margaux, a painter dealing with similar issues. The book also focused on Sheila's relationship with Israel, a manipulative and charismatic lover, as well as her ambition to complete a play she had been commissioned to write. The book was a collage of many elements, including transcripts of conversations, emails, recordings, dreams, and fancies, which were sometimes altered, fabricated, or verbatim.

How Should a Person Be? was a work that challenged and expanded on the autofiction genre, which Heti had previously explored in her works, The Middle Stories and The Middle Voice. How Should a Person Be? Heti blurred the boundaries between fact and fiction, reality and imagination, and self and other to an unprecedented degree, resulting in a hybrid genre she referred to as "a novel from life." She also questioned the nature and purpose of writing, as well as the writer's duty and obligation to oneself, others, and the world. She also experimented with other styles of expression, including comedy, tragedy, poetry, and theater.

How Should a Person Be? was a book that had a significant impact on the literary scene, both in Canada and around the world. It received rave reviews and was selected as book of the year by a number of magazines, including The New York Times Book Review, The New Yorker, and The Guardian. It was also a finalist for the renowned Women's Prize for Fiction and received the Believer Book Award. It was translated into various languages and sold more than 100,000 copies worldwide. It has inspired and impacted numerous writers, including Lena Dunham,

Rachel Cusk, and Jenny Offill, who recognized Heti's contributions to the autofiction genre as well as the representation of women's lives and voices in literary works.

How Should a Person Be? was likewise a work that received divided and controversial reactions from reviewers and readers, who either commended, panned, or both. Some journalists and readers praised Heti's uniqueness and honesty, calling her work invigorating and relatable. They admired her wit and humor, her insight and knowledge, as well as her bravery and sensitivity. They also appreciated her talent, expertise, vision, and voice, as well as her drive and success. They recognized her as a writer who was not afraid to take chances and question norms, and who had something essential and relevant to say. For example, James Wood of The New Yorker described Heti as "a major writer" and her work as "a vital and funny picture of the excitements and longueurs of trying to be a young creator in a free, late-capitalist Western city.".

Some critics and readers, however, were turned off by Heti's self-indulgence and narcissism, finding her work unpleasant and arrogant. They complained about her lack of storyline and organization, her excessive navel-gazing and triviality, and her lack of morality and empathy. They also questioned her genuineness and reliability, her manner and method, as well as her goal and message. They regarded her as a writer who was overly self-absorbed and self-conscious, with nothing meaningful or fresh to offer. For example, Adam Kirsch, writing for The New Republic, described Heti as "a bad writer" and her book as "a document of the novel's failure to engage with the world.".

How should a person be? In short, it was a masterpiece that transformed both the contemporary novel and Sheila Heti's writing. It was a piece that posed a simple yet profound question and provided a nuanced and provocative response. It was a piece that made a statement, provoked a debate, made an impression, and left a lasting legacy. It was through his work that he became a writer.

Chapter 7

THE METAPHYSICAL POLL: A COLLABORATION EXPERIMENT

Sheila Heti's fourth book, The Metaphysical Poll (2008), was a collaborative experiment with hundreds of people from around the United States. It was a site that compiled and interpreted people's sleeping nightmares concerning Hillary Clinton and Barack Obama during the 2008 Democratic primary. It was also a book that examined and commented on the dreams, as well as what they showed about the country's political and psychological state.

Sheila Heti's inspiration for The Metaphysical Poll stemmed from her passion for dreams and curiosity about the collective unconscious. She wondered what type of fantasies people had about the two candidates, who were both historic and iconic personalities with opposing ideas and values for the country. She was also curious about what the dreams would reveal about the American people's ambitions and anxieties, desires and conflicts, fantasies, and reality.

Sheila Heti's strategy for The Metaphysical Poll was straightforward and inventive. She started a blog and asked people to submit their dreams about Clinton and Obama, along with some basic information like their name, age, gender, locality, and political preferences. She then shared the dreams on her blog, along with her own commentary and interpretations based on intuition and study. She also divided the dreams into other themes, including sex, violence, family, race, and religion.

Sheila Heti's results for The Metaphysical Poll were both shocking and illuminating. She got hundreds of dreams from people of various origins, ages, and perspectives who offered intimate and unusual images of the candidates. The dreams varied from normal and commonplace to strange and fanciful, hilarious, and bizarre. Some of the dreams were nice and supportive, while others were negative and hostile, or ambiguous and conflicted. Some of the dreams were prophetic and correct, while others were sardonic and contradicting, or cryptic and unfathomable.

Sheila Heti's study and reflections on The Metaphysical Poll were fascinating and challenging. She investigated the dreams' interpretations and consequences, as well as what they revealed and concealed about the applicants. She also investigated the connections and inconsistencies between dreams and reality, as well as how they interacted and influenced one another. She also questioned the dreams' role and purpose, whether they provided insight or illusion, guidance or confusion, liberation or limitation.

Sheila Heti's impact and influence on The Metaphysical Poll were considerable and long-lasting. She developed a one-of-a-kind and original work of art and literature that united the personal and political, the individual and the collective, the subjective and objective. She also ignited a conversation and a debate, engaging and challenging readers and journalists, who either complimented or condemned her idea. She also predicted the results of the primaries and Obama's victory as president based on the dreams she gathered and interpreted.

Chapter 8

MOTHERHOOD INK

Motherhood was not an intermission in Heti's literary exploration. It was a seismic change—a tectonic plate reshaping the landscape of her career and life. Motherhood, for Heti, was not a neatly penned chapter in a Hallmark greeting card; it was a messy, complex experience full of inconsistencies and doubts, a stark contrast to the mainstream narrative of motherhood. And, much as her pen had unraveled the strands of selfhood and relationships in her previous works, she approached parenthood with unwavering honesty and naked vulnerability.

Sheila Heti's sixth book, Motherhood (2018), was a deep and profound exploration of the decision to have or not have children, as well as the repercussions for a woman's life and creativity. It was also a contentious and bold work that called into question societal expectations and constraints on women, as well as redefining the maternal narrative in literature and society.

Motherhood was inspired by Heti's own life and experiences, as well as those of her friends and family, who shared their insights and stories with her. The book followed the protagonist, Sheila, a writer in her late thirties who was uncertain and conflicted about having a child. The book also included her partner, Miles, who was supportive but uninterested, and her mother, who was disappointed but polite. The book featured a collage of many materials, such as journal entries, coin tosses, tarot readings, and dreams, which were sometimes true, sometimes fiction, and sometimes ambiguous.

"Motherhood," she asserted in "Motherhood: A Novel," "is the least interesting thing about a woman." This wasn't an attack on mothers; it was a rebellion against society's oppressive expectations and the glossy veneer of perfection that it imposes on the experience. Heti dared to pull back the veil, revealing the complex contrasts beneath: tiredness, frustration, inner ambivalence, and seething hatred toward a job that is frequently glorified but rarely actually understood.

She didn't hide from the visceral facts, the bodily upheavals, or the hormonal storms that threatened to consume her. She described the milky haze of new motherhood—the desperate search for her own identity in the middle of another's constant wants. She described the remorse as the nagging feeling of failing every expectation, both internal and external. This wasn't a confession; it was a collective sigh of relief, a permission slip for other mothers to see the flaws in the facade, the darkness alongside the light.

But Heti's examination of parenthood extended beyond the bodily and emotional. She dug into philosophy, challenging the basic core of this societal institution. Why, she wondered, must women sacrifice so much of themselves to become mothers? Why is our value dependent on our ability to nurture others? She challenged the inflexible binary of career vs. motherhood, as well as the tacit idea that women must choose between personal fulfillment and family life. And she dared to venture into the forbidden terrain of maternal ambivalence, the difficult truth that not every woman is filled with maternal instinct and that not every mother treasures every minute.

This unprecedented honesty, this willingness to disclose the darker side of motherhood, was more than a personal catharsis; it was a cultural earthquake. Heti, with her trademark blend of wit and reflection, gave voice to a generation of mothers who felt silenced, their experiences deemed inappropriate for polite speech. In doing so, she demolished the myth of the flawless, selfless mother, providing a more nuanced and authentic depiction of motherhood that resonated with women all around the world.

"Motherhood," Heti eventually confessed, "is like becoming an ocean: boundless, vast, terrifying, and beautiful." Her work on this theme was not a rejection of motherhood; rather, it was a reclamation of it, a redefining on her own terms. It was a dirty, honest, and truly human depiction of this common experience, reminding us that even in the midst of diapers and tantrums, the poetry of parenthood can exist, not in an idealized version but in the raw, vulnerable truth of it all.

Motherhood was a work that extended and built on the autofiction genre, which Heti had mastered in prior works like How Should a Person Be? and The Middle Voice. Heti blurred the boundaries between fact and fiction, reality and imagination, and self and other to an even greater extent in Motherhood, resulting in a hybrid genre she referred to as "a novel from life." She also questioned the nature and purpose of writing, as well as the writer's duty and obligation to oneself, others, and the world. She also experimented with other styles of expression, including comedy, tragedy, poetry, and philosophy.

Motherhood has had a significant impact on the literary scene in Canada and around the world. It received rave reviews and was selected as book of the year by a number of magazines, including The New York Times Book Review, The New Yorker, and The Guardian. It was also a finalist for the prestigious Giller Prize in Canada and received the Believer Book Award in the United States. It was translated into various languages and sold more than 50,000 copies globally. It has inspired and impacted numerous writers, including Sally Rooney, Jia Tolentino, and Kristen Roupenian, who recognized Heti's contribution to the autofiction genre as well as the representation of women's lives and perspectives in literature.

Motherhood received varied and divisive reviews from critics and readers, who either applauded it, condemned it, or both. Some journalists and readers praised Heti's uniqueness and honesty, calling her work invigorating and relatable. They admired her wit and humor, her insight and knowledge, as well as her bravery and sensitivity. They also appreciated her talent, expertise, vision, and voice, as well as her drive and success. They recognized her as a writer who was not afraid to take chances and question norms, and who had something essential and relevant to say. Lauren Oyler of The Baffler praised Heti as a "great writer" and her work as "a vital and funny exploration of the most consequential decision of early adulthood.

Some critics and readers, however, were turned off by Heti's self-indulgence and narcissism, finding her work unpleasant and arrogant. They complained about her lack of storyline and organization, her excessive navel-gazing and triviality, and her lack of morality and empathy. They also questioned her genuineness and reliability, her manner and method, as well as her goal and message. They regarded her as a writer who was overly self-absorbed and self-conscious, with nothing meaningful or fresh to offer. Adam Kirsch, writing for The Atlantic, branded Heti "a bad writer" and her book "a document of the failure of the novel to engage with the world."

Heti's discovery of motherhood was more than just a chapter in her own tale; it was a chapter in the lives of every woman who has ever struggled with the difficulties of this role. It was a fracture in the immaculate mask, a call to recognize the whole range of emotions, the doubts and joys, and the challenges and successes that comprise the tapestry of motherhood. And it demonstrated the capacity of literature to uncover the darkest corners of human existence, to unite us in our shared vulnerability, and to rewrite the narratives that limit us.

In short, Motherhood redefined the maternal story and Sheila Heti's writing. It was a piece that posed a simple yet profound question and provided a nuanced and provocative response. It was a piece that made a statement, provoked a debate, made an impression, and left a lasting legacy.

Chapter 9

THE DIGITAL FRONTIER

Sheila Heti's writing has always been affected by and sensitive to the digital age, including the opportunities and problems it brings to artists and intellectuals. She has embraced technology as a tool for creating, communicating, and cooperating, establishing new online communities and platforms that encourage conversation, experimentation, and diversity. She has also investigated how technology affects human character, conduct, and creativity, as well as the limits and potential of human-machine interaction.

Heti has incorporated technology into her work by including online components and forms, including emails, blogs, surveys, and chatbots, in her books and essays. She's also used the internet for inspiration and research, incorporating online content like search results, news articles, and social media posts into her writing. She has stated that she appreciates using the internet as a "randomizer" and the serendipity and surprise of discovering unexpected connections and information online. She has also stated that she views the internet as a "library" and that she enjoys learning from and citing the works and ideas of others.

Heti's online activity extends beyond her writing. She is also active and influential on social media platforms like Twitter, Instagram, and Goodreads, where she offers her ideas, opinions, and recommendations while engaging with her readers and followers. She has also experimented with various forms of social media, such as starting a blog called The Metaphysical Poll, where she collected and analyzed people's dreams about Hillary Clinton and Barack Obama during the 2008 US presidential primaries, and working with an AI chatbot named Alice, which resulted in a short story published in The New Yorker. She has stated that she is interested in using social media to explore and express herself, as well as engage with and learn from others.

Heti's online presence is also reflected in her establishment and participation in a variety of online communities and projects aimed at encouraging and supporting artistic and intellectual interaction and innovation. She has worked as an editor, writer, and interviewer for online magazines and publications such as The Believer, McSweeney's, and n+1, contributing to and curating a variety of topics and features. She has also developed and curated Trampoline Hall, a monthly lecture series that involves speakers who improvise on themes outside of their fields of expertise, which has been held both in person and virtually. She has also worked with other writers and artists, including Leanne Shapton, Heidi Julavits, Miranda July, and Misha Glouberman, to create online projects such as Women in Clothes, a website and book that examines how women think about what they wear, and Learning to Talk to Yourself, a website and podcast that investigates the art and practice of self-talk.

Heti's involvement with technology and the digital frontier demonstrates her curiosity and courage. She has demonstrated a remarkable capacity and willingness to adapt, experiment, and develop with many kinds of technology, as well as to create and participate in online communities and platforms that enrich and challenge her artistic and intellectual endeavors. She has also demonstrated a strong interest in and understanding of the effects and implications of technology on human character, conduct, and creativity, as well as a willingness to challenge and investigate the limits and possibilities of human-machine interaction. She is the true voice of the new vanguard.

Chapter 10

THE BIRTH OF TRAMPOLINE HALL

Sheila Heti has always been interested in establishing and promoting forums for alternative voices, as well as encouraging dialogue and experimentation among different and curious minds. Trampoline Hall, a monthly lecture series she established and managed in Toronto in 2001, has subsequently moved to New York and other locations. Trampoline Hall is a one-of-a-kind and entertaining event in which speakers are invited to discuss topics outside of their areas of expertise, and the audience is encouraged to ask questions and challenge the presenters. The end result is a lively and spontaneous interchange of ideas, opinions, and stories that honors the uniqueness and ingenuity of human invention.

Trampoline Hall sprang from Heti's frustration with the traditional and dull lecture forms she saw throughout her studies and profession. She wanted to develop a lecture series that was more entertaining, participatory, and democratic, where anyone could speak on any topic and the audience could contribute and learn from one another. She also wanted to create a venue where individuals could discuss things about which they were interested or passionate but lacked official credentials or authority. She believed that this would allow for more unique and honest opinions, as well as show gaps and limitations in expert knowledge.

Heti asked her friend Misha Glouberman, an improv teacher and consultant, to host and moderate the event, as well as offer advice and comments to the speakers. She also requested that other members of her creative and intellectual circles serve as curators, selecting the speakers and topics for each show. Curators featured writers, artists, singers, comedians, and campaigners such as Margaux Williamson, Life of a Craphead, and Xenia Benivolski. The speakers included professors, journalists, students, bartenders, celebrities, and politicians. The subjects ranged from the history of 3D to suicide notes, cultural entropy in the internet era, the perfect baguette, and being an asshole.

Trampoline Hall immediately became a popular and acclaimed event, drawing big and enthusiastic crowds and receiving great feedback from publications such as The New Yorker, The Village Voice, and The Globe and Mail. In 2002, it embarked on a 10-city tour of the United States, performing in New York and San Francisco on multiple occasions. It has also sparked spin-offs and imitations in other cities and countries, including London, Berlin, and Sydney. In

2017, Heti and Glouberman developed a podcast version of Trampoline Hall, which includes recordings of previous lectures and conversations with the speakers.

Trampoline Hall is more than simply a lecture series. It is a community and movement that challenges and enriches contemporary culture and discourse. It is a platform for alternative voices, providing a voice and visibility to people and issues that are frequently disregarded or underrepresented by mainstream media and academia. It is also a forum for discussion and experimentation, stimulating and satisfying the curiosity and creativity of both presenters and audience members. It is one of Haiti's most unique and impactful contributions to the literary and creative arenas.

Chapter 11

THE FUTURE OF THE NEW VANGUARD

Sheila Heti's literary passion extends far beyond the pages of her own works. Her work, like a Molotov cocktail thrown at the staid walls of conventional narrative, sparked a wildfire of "New Vanguard" writing, which is defined by its unflinching embrace of the personal, genre-bending fluidity, and raw exploration of the anxieties and absurdities of contemporary life. But Heti's legacy is more than simply a single moment in literary history; it is a torch she has passed down to a new generation of writers who are transforming the landscape of fiction in their own radical ways.

Among these torchbearers is Ocean Vuong, whose debut novel "On Earth, We're Briefly Gorgeous" combines lyrical and autofiction to create a moving portrait of queer Vietnamese American identity. Ottessa Moshfegh's darkly comedic stories, such as "Eileen" and "McGlue," mock societal expectations with a razor-sharp wit that echoes Heti's own daring irreverence. Then there's Rachel Cusk, whose "Outline" trilogy deconstructs the novel's core form, asking readers to confront the gaps and silences of autobiography in the same manner that Heti did with "How to Be a Person in the World."

These are just a few names from a constellation of talents, each with their own distinct brilliance. What unifies them is not just Heti's influence but also their shared audacity to break the mold, to deconstruct outdated literary traditions, and to mine the depths of themselves with unwavering honesty. They challenge genre conventions, blurring the lines between fiction and reality, memoir and essay, and generating works that are as much about the act of creation as the lives they portray.

But the New Vanguard's progress is more than just a continuation of Heti's pioneering work. It's a kaleidoscope of voices and perspectives that continually shift and resist easy categorization. Writers such as Carmen Maria Machado are reworking magical realism for the digital age, while Jenny Offill's fragmentary narratives depict the splintered reality of modern life. Meanwhile, Alexandra Kleeman creates disturbing dystopias that eerily reflect our own concerns about technology and monitoring.

One of the most fascinating characteristics of this literary movement is its acceptance of hybridity. The days of tight genre divisions are over. Heti's torchbearers thrive in the tangled intersection of formats, weaving poetry into prose, injecting essays with memoiristic aspects, and creating graphic novels that transcend categorization. This genre-bending fluidity reflects the complexities of modern life, in which the distinctions between the personal and the political, the actual and the imaginary, are continuously blurred.

Despite their stylistic differences, these various voices have a common thread. It is a dedication to vulnerability, to exposing the tangled paradoxes of oneself without apologies. Heti's influence can be seen in their willingness to confront the worries and insecurities that lurk behind the surface of ordinary life and to wrestle with the uncertainties of relationships, careers, and the very purpose of existence.

The New Vanguard is more than simply a blip on the literary radar; it represents a paradigm change in how we create tales and make sense of the world. It's a movement that dares to be untidy, honest, and completely human. At its core, it retains the indelible imprint of Sheila Heti, the creative rebel who dared to break the rules and write life on her own terms.

However, the saga of the New Vanguard is far from over. Every day, new voices emerge, each contributing a unique note to the symphony of contemporary literature. Heti's flame is still being passed down, paving the way for a new generation of writers who are willing to break down barriers and reinvent what it means to tell a tale. As these torchbearers stretch the frontiers of autofiction, genre-bending, and uncensored honesty, the New Vanguard's future looks as daring and unpredictable as the world it depicts.

Sheila Heti's legacy extends beyond the pages of her own works. It lives on via the voices of those she has inspired, the blurring of genres, and the brave exploration of the self that her work has sparked. The New Vanguard, permanently defined by her revolutionary spirit, will continue to burn a trail of literary fire, illuminating the ever-changing landscape of contemporary literature for years.

Chapter 12

THE ALICE MUNRO CHAIR OF CREATIVITY: A PRESTIGIOUS APPOINTMENT

Sheila Heti's writing has gained her numerous accolades and awards, but none are as distinguished and valuable as the Alice Munro Chair of Creativity at Western University in London, Ontario. This post, named after the Nobel Prize-winning Canadian writer and Western alumna, celebrates and honors Heti's outstanding achievements and contributions to the literary and creative worlds, as well as providing her with the chance to mentor and inspire a new generation of writers and thinkers.

The Alice Munro Chair of Creativity was established in 2016 with the cooperation and agreement of Alice Munro, who is one of Western's most distinguished alumni. Munro's first connection to Western's Department of English occurred in 1949, when she enrolled as an undergraduate majoring in English and soon after had her first publication in Folio, a campus literary magazine. She was Western's third Writer-in-Residence in 1974, and in 1976, Western bestowed an honorary degree on Munro for her literary achievements, the only one she has ever received. Munro received the Nobel Prize in Literature in 2013 for being a "master of the contemporary short story.".

The Alice Munro Chair of Creativity is a full-time, limited-term appointment lasting one to three years, with an academic rank commensurate with the successful candidate's qualifications. The position is located at the Department of English and Writing Studies, or as a joint appointment between English and Writing Studies and another department in the Faculty of Arts and Humanities, as suitable. The successful candidate is expected to maintain a strong creative and research program while also educating undergraduates, graduate students, and postdoctoral fellows. The post also entails leading the university's relationship with the local creative community as well as delivering the annual Alice Munro Lecture on Creativity.

Heti was named Alice Munro Chair of Creativity in 2023, succeeding previous holders Ivan Coyote, an award-winning playwright and theatrical performer, and Nino Ricci, an acclaimed novelist and former president of PEN Canada. Heti's selection was greeted with joy and admiration from the Western community and beyond, since she was widely regarded as one of the most innovative and influential writers of her time, as well as a suitable successor to Munro's legacy. Heti's novels have been published abroad and translated into twenty-five languages. The New York Times named her "The New Vanguard," and The Washington Post ranked her as one of the best living authors. She has also received numerous accolades, including the Governor General's Literary Award for Fiction, the Vine Award for Canadian Jewish Literature, and the KM Hunter Artists Award.

Heti's stint as the Alice Munro Chair of Creativity has been distinguished by her active and generous participation in the creative culture of the Faculty of Arts and Humanities, as well as her innovative and inspiring teaching and mentorship of students and faculty. She has taken graduate and undergraduate courses, workshops, and seminars where she has shared her knowledge and experiences with numerous aspects of writing and creativity, including genre, form, style, voice, and process. She has also supported and promoted students' and faculty's creative work by offering criticism, direction, and opportunities for publishing and presentation. She has also worked with various departments and programs, including Religious Studies, Philosophy, and Visual Arts, to encourage multidisciplinary and cross-cultural communication and interaction.

Heti has also taken on a leadership position between the university and the local creative community, organizing and participating in a number of events and projects that highlight and promote the diversity and vitality of artistic expression and appreciation. She has improved and enlarged the Writer-in-Residence program by inviting and hosting international authors and artists, including Elena Ferrante, Agnes Varda, and Sophie Calle, to lecture and collaborate. She has also continued and curated her renowned and acclaimed lecture series, Trampoline Hall, which is held both in person and online and invites speakers to speak on topics outside of their fields of expertise, with the audience encouraged to ask questions and challenge the presenters. She has also given the annual Alice Munro Lecture on Creativity, where she discussed fate and chance, memory and imagination, and art and experience.

Heti's nomination as the Alice Munro Chair of Creativity recognizes her artistic vision and excellence, as well as her dedication to utilizing her writing to explore, question, and transform herself and the world. She has honored and copied Munro's legacy by establishing and promoting forums for unusual and diverse views, as well as encouraging dialogue and experimentation among curious and creative minds. She has also inspired and impacted a new generation of authors and intellectuals, who regard her as a mentor and role model and hope to follow in her footsteps in the literary and artistic fields. She is the true voice of the new vanguard.

Chapter 13

BEYOND WORDS: SHEILA HETI'S LASTING LEGACY

Sheila Heti is more than just a writer; she is a cultural seismograph, constantly recording the tremors and upheavals beneath the surface of modern life. Her work, which spans genres and defies easy categorization, has not only transformed the literary landscape but has also challenged our fundamental assumptions about reading, writing, and living. Her legacy is inscribed not only in ink on paper but also in the minds and emotions of readers who recognize their own concerns, wants, and vulnerabilities in her unflinchingly honest work.

One of Heti's most important contributions is her radicalization of the intimate. By blurring the barriers between fiction and autobiography, she has given a generation of writers the freedom to examine themselves with candor and sensitivity. Heti's work celebrates the complexity, paradoxes, and raw honesty of real experience rather than the sanitized, fictionalized narratives of the past. In doing so, she has not only liberated writers but also created a generation of readers who are sensitive to the subtle complexity of the self and the world around them.

Beyond straightforward honesty, Heti's art promotes a conversational, intimate tone. Her work feels like a buddy sharing secrets over coffee, drawing the reader into a shared place of trust and discovery. This intimacy generates a distinct empathy, removing traditional barriers between author and audience and forming a community of readers who feel seen, understood, and linked.

Furthermore, Heti's whimsical exploration of form has disrupted the traditional conventions of storytelling. From the fragmentary essays of "How Should a Person Be?" to the joint memoir-manifesto "Motherhood: Stories From Women Who Don't Have Children," she resists categorization, opening new paths and motivating others to follow suit. This genre-bending approach represents life's varied nature, refusing to be limited by standard literary genres.

But Heti's legacy goes well beyond aesthetics. Her work dives into some of today's most serious issues: modern-day worries, interpersonal complexity, and the search for meaning in a society inundated with noise. She creates a space for thought and discourse by addressing these issues with honesty and humor, establishing a sense of community understanding and solidarity in the face of common uncertainties.

Perhaps most importantly, Heti's work reminds us that life is a never-ending experiment. By challenging conventional standards, embracing vulnerability, and playing with form, she inspires us to do the same—to become active participants in our own narratives and rewrite the rules of our existence.

Of course, Heti's legacy is not without criticism. Some see her writing as self-indulgent, while others question the distinction between memoir and fiction. Her impact, however, is defined by her determination to push limits and face criticism. Heti is not a writer looking for comfort or unanimity; she is a provocateur, a conversation starter, and a mirror reflecting a generation's worries and wants.

To summarize, Sheila Heti's legacy is defined not by honors or plaudits but by the enormous impact she made on readers and authors alike. She has broken down barriers and demonstrated that literature is more than simply entertainment; it can be a tool for self-discovery, connection, and transformation. As long as readers find refuge and challenge in her unabashed honesty, genre-bending innovation, and dedication to the intimate, her writings will reverberate, whispering their stories long after the last page is turned. Her legacy is not a static monument but rather a live discussion that invites us to join her in the ongoing production of our own literary and personal stories. The genuine measure of her long-term impact is found in that continuous conversation.

EPILOGUE

THE WORLD IN HETI'S WORDS

As we come to the end of Sheila Heti's literary voyage, it's easy to anticipate a final conclusion—a great summary of her impact. But Heti, ever the renegade, resists such easy resolution. Her legacy is more than just a nicely bound volume on a shelf; it's a real, breathing discourse with a ripple effect that touches innumerable lives in subtle and profound ways.

To suggest that she has altered the way we read and write is almost reductive. Heti has dug deeper, redefining how we see ourselves, negotiate relationships, and deal with the absurdities of life. Her writings have launched not only a literary movement but also a cultural upheaval, inspiring a generation to accept vulnerability, question standards, and experiment with the very fabric of their existence.

Heti's influence is as varied as the voices she has inspired. The naked honesty of Ocean Vuong's poetry, Rachel Cusk's fragmentary narratives, and Ottessa Moshfegh's darkly comedic wit all demonstrate this. But it's not only about these literary torchbearers; it's also about the innumerable readers who find consolation and challenge in her work, who have learned to question narratives, embrace messiness, and create their own stories with renewed confidence.

Her legacy is not limited to the printed page. It spills over into café talks, scribbled notes in journals, and whispered confessions amongst pals. It's in the silent act of choosing authenticity over perfection, in the bravery to defy conventional standards and build one's own way.

And, while trends come and go, Heti's central message remains: life is a messy, continuing experiment. There are no clear answers or elegant solutions. However, inside that chaos is the opportunity for meaningful connection, self-discovery, and development. Heti's work does not provide answers, rather, it encourages us to ask questions, embrace the unknown, and celebrate the lovely imperfection of being human.

So, as we approach the final page, let us refrain from seeking a clear conclusion. Instead, let us enjoy the ongoing conversation that Heti has sparked. Allow her words to reverberate in our minds, encouraging us to question, examine, and rewrite our own life stories. By doing so, we preserve her legacy, not as a monument to the past but as a vibrant invitation to co-create the future, one honest, messy, magnificently incomplete chapter at a time.

The universe appears to be slowly being rebuilt, in Heti's words: vulnerability, experimentation, and an unwavering pursuit of the real self. And, within that ever-changing story, her eternal legacy will continue to shine, serving as a source of inspiration for future generations.

15 LIFE-CHANGING HETI HACKS INSPIRED BY SHEILA HETI

Forget self-help platitudes: Sheila Heti's work isn't about living a picture-perfect life. It's about embracing the magnificent complexity of life, challenging the status quo, and generating social, mental, and personal breakthroughs from within. So, get off the self-improvement treadmill and buckle up for 15 Heti-inspired hacks that will rock your world:

- 1. Stop hiding your "flaws." Every Monday, set aside an hour to share your true thoughts and feelings with a friend, family member, or even a trustworthy stranger. You'll be astonished at how this vulnerability fosters deeper connections.

- 2. Genre-Bending Brunch: Are you tired of predictable dates? Schedule a "genre-bending brunch" with a friend. Each of you writes a story prompt on a napkin before switching to create a short piece in an entirely different style. Share and giggle at your literary mash-ups!

- 3. Norm-Smashing Challenge: Choose a social norm that bothers you. For a week, subtly disrupt it with your behaviors. Write a poem from the perspective of your "unruly" self, or engage in a courteous discourse with someone who represents the norm, challenging their viewpoint.

- 4. Perfectionism sucks! Start an "Unfinished Masterpiece Club" with your pals. Choose a creative project without any expectations. Paint for 15 minutes, write a scene without editing, compose a song with nonsense lyrics—the idea is to enjoy the process of creation rather than the pressure of a finished output.

- 5. Motherhood Redefined: Whether you're a parent, childfree, or navigating societal expectations, explore your unique relationship with "motherhood." Write a letter to your younger self about it, have a conversation with someone who disagrees, or create art reflecting your personal perspective.

- 6. Curiosity Convo: Avoid small talk! The next time you meet someone new, ask open-ended questions like "What's your wildest dream?" or "What's your most unpopular opinion?" Accept awkward silences and relish the delight of genuine human connection.

- 7. Identity Deconstruction Party: Invite your pals to a lighthearted identity discovery party! Write down the labels with which you identify, and then dispute each one. Play games, conduct discussions, and celebrate your ever-changing identity.

- 8. Gratitude Graffiti: Discover the beauty in the mundane! Take a walk and write down five things you usually ignore, such as a broken sidewalk, a child's laughter, and the smell of rain. Write them as "gratitude graffiti" on a public surface (with permission!) or send them to loved ones.

- 9. Genre-Mash Mashup: Write a flash fiction story combining a grocery list, a love letter, and a news item. Push your creative limitations and explore the surprising possibilities of storytelling.

- 10. Friendship Manifesto Workshop: Gather your squad and embrace your inner Heti! Discuss your ideals, desires, and what makes your friendships special. Create a "Friendship Manifesto" describing your desire for deeper ties, and then celebrate with fun and shared dreams.

- 11. "No" is Your Superpower: Consider a situation in which you struggle to decline. Role-play saying "no" with a buddy, practice forceful but gentle refusals, and prioritize things that are actually important to you. Remember: boundaries are wonderful!

- 12. Failure Fiesta: Failure is a fertilizer! Reflect on a previous "flop" and find the hidden lessons. Throw a "failure fiesta" with your friends, write a funny song about it, or make art that reclaims the story. Remember that growth may be messy, humorous, and empowering.

- 13. Reclaim Your Creative Muse: Dust off that discarded paintbrush or silent keyboard! Dedicate 15 minutes per day to revisiting a previously ignored creative pursuit. Do not pass judgment; instead, create. You could be amazed at the hidden talents that emerge.

- 14. Digital Detox Dinner: Do you feel overwhelmed by online noise? Plan a "digital detox dinner" with pals. Leave your phones at the door, focus on the present moment, and have real talks. Rediscover the simple delight of being human while unplugged.

- 15. Live Your Heti Legacy: Begin each day by setting an aim, no matter how big or small. Maintain consciousness throughout your actions, celebrate progress, and change direction as needed. Remember that life is a Heti-like adventure, not a pre-written script. Accept the clutter, the questions, and the thrill of co-creating your own unique story.

These are simply sparks to start your Heti-inspired adventure. As you learn more about her work and your own life, keep in mind that transformation is rarely linear. Embrace the stumbles.

Charles Cartwright

Printed in Great Britain
by Amazon